The Great Big Success Quote Book: Over 501 Powerful Quotes on Wealth, Wisdom, Work & More!

Compiled by Cameron M. Clark

Book 3 in 'The Great Big Quote Books' Series

The Great Big Success Quote Book: Over
501 Powerful Quotes on Wealth, Wisdom,
Work & More!

Published by Paul St. George Press

Email: greatbigquotebooks@gmail.com

ISBN-13:

978-1523420735

ISBN-10:

1523420731

Preface

When I first published 'The Great Big Success Quote Book' as solely a Kindle eBook, I'd compared success and failure to a beautiful woman and a harsh teacher respectively.

In less than a year, I've been schooled and I have had my understanding of what it is to be forced to stand at the edge of the precipice of failure and to not know if and when success would reappear. Needless to say, this last year's experiences have deepened my appreciation and understanding of these two life elements more powerfully than I'd ever imagined possible.

I still believe what I wrote a year ago when this book was first published.

However, I want to share with you what has been on my mind for the last 12 months. Since writing the original preface for this book, I feel that life, the universe or some other overriding supernatural force greater than myself has desired to teach me a new lesson.

Through no choice of my own, I was faced with some of the greatest, ongoing professional challenges I've ever known. It is possible that these trials might be intended to provide a deeper meaning behind the words Success and Failure. This yearlong lesson has come with some suffering and uncertainty. It's also been punctuated with moments of happiness and relief. Other times, the trials were ongoing.

I have begun to understand the stanza from Rudyard Kipling's poem 'If' more deeply than I ever had in all my years of living prior to this new education:

If you can meet with Triumph and Disaster

And treat those two impostors just the same;

I won't diminish the simple elegance of the above passage with some personal interpretation of it, other than to say that to me, those have been the most valuable words in the entire poem (which I have committed to memory at the time of this writing). At the risk of personal vulnerability, I will admit to you that Kipling's advice and observations in 'If' along with the many other insights he gives in the poem have carried me through some of the darkest times of my life.

We can't control all of the bad things that come into our lives. Some things we can prevent, but we can't control all of the bad events. If we could, there would never be any suffering in the world and everyone would be millionaires. There would also be little growth and learning, I presume. When bad things happen, whether it is disease, divorce, dissolution of wealth or some other event we could not foresee, we don't really have a lot of choice of whether or not to avoid them. Instead, the only choice we really have is how we will act and react in those situations.

Will we whither and shrink in the face of a new, seemingly overwhelming trial or will we round up our shoulders, stiffen our collective upper lip and press forward into the fire with a determination to get to the other unseen side of this difficulty?

I can't say I have faced every trial perfectly this last year with the determined visage I had just described. I don't think that's the point though. I think the key to a lot of this is to endure. It's to look for ways to overcome these challenges and to more fully appreciate felicity when it makes its temporary return.

vi

Anyway, here's to health, wealth and happiness for you and yours as you continue down this path toward your dreams and goals.

Cameron M. Clark

June 2016

Contents

Preface...iii

Contents vii

Introduction x

Invitation xii

Acknowledgements............................ xv

Accountability 16

Action...18

Adversity..20

Ambition..21

Attitude..22

Authority..23

Change 24

Character..25

Commitment......................................26

Communication 27

Confidence 29

Conquering Fear 30

Courage 31

Creativity 33

Dealing with Failure 36

Decision-Making 38

Determination....................................40

Discipline 42

viii

Dreams 44

Education 45

Enthusiasm 49

Entrepreneurship 51

Ethics 52

Focus 53

Goal Setting 54

Habits 57

Ideas 58

Imagination 59

Innovation 60

Integrity 61

Knowledge 63

Leadership 64

Listening 66

Luck 67

Management 69

Motivation 70

Opportunity 72

Overcoming Obstacles 74

Perseverance 78

Persistence 80

Planning 82

Positive Thinking 84

Preparation 88

Problem Solving 90

Progress 92

Purpose...94

Responsibility 96

Results 99

Risk Taking 101

Sacrifice..104

Self-Control...106

Self Improvement.......................................108

Selling..111

Service...113

Simplicity...115

Success 117

Talent 120

Teamwork..122

Thoughts...123

Time Management 125

Vision 127

Wealth..129

Wisdom..131

Work 134

About the Compiler 138

Introduction

Just as you found in 'The Great Big Fitness Quote Book' and 'The Great Big Love Quote Book,' this book contains quotations that are mainly taken from credible people who have achieved a recognizable measure of Success in at least one area of their lives and careers. Inside you will find the wisdom and advice of world-renowned Scientists, world-champion Athletes, accomplished Entrepreneurs, insightful Writers and Philosophers and many others who come from the varied walks of life.

In compiling this book, I tried to avoid quoting anyone whose *only* claim to Success is making a living teaching other people how to live. There are a number of those types out there and I felt they really served little purpose in this book.

Who could offer more value to you and your life than an individual who worked in their chosen profession with all of the grit, guts and determination it took to get to where he or she wanted to be?

I think people like Oprah Winfrey, Thomas Edison, Anita Roddick, General Colin Powell, Bruce Lee, Margaret Thatcher, Steve Jobs and many others, who've had to persevere through difficulty and trial speak with true credibility. There are also those who've made the study of Success one of their lifetime pursuits: Malcolm Gladwell, Tom Rath, Brian Tracy and Stephen R. Covey to name a few. I think you will be happy with the variety of men and women featured in this book. All have been vetted and include at least one occupation the quoted individual spent time doing during his or her lifetime.

I am grateful to many of those who have gone before me and I know that their wisdom and experience can help you as it has helped me.

Invitation

Like the book? I'd love a review!

Feel free to give your feedback on www.Amazon.com to let others know what you thought about this book. As you know, there are some things I really tried to do different with this than a lot of the other quote books you find on Amazon that seem to just be a random quick copy-and-paste style collection of quotes so prevalent online.

Also, if you want more information on 'The Great Big Quote Books' series, you can 'like' us on Facebook by clicking: https://www.facebook.com/greatbigquotebo oks. I will be posting many quotes on Fitness, Love & Success that you can share with your friends through social media.

You can also follow us on Instagram where various memes are posted from time to time on the below subjects! Check out @greatbigquotebooks there.

'The Great Big Love Quote Book' and 'The Great Big Fitness Quote Book' are also on sale at Amazon.com.

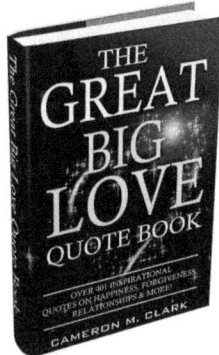 

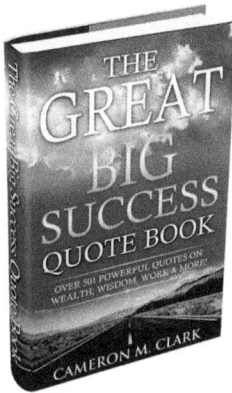

Thanks again for reading!

One More Thing:

If you liked the electronic versions of the books, but you want an analog copy of one or all to take to the beach or give as a gift, I have great news!

They're also now available in print form either through Amazon or CreateSpace. Check them out!

Acknowledgements

This book wouldn't be possible without the encouragement of my wife, Cara.

I also want to thank my kids for their love and support. They spur me forward toward greater success and a more powerful desire to achieve my goals.

I also want to thank my other family members, friends and those with whom I have worked professionally for many years. I have learned much more from you than I think you could ever gain from me.

To my publisher, Paul St. George Press, I want to thank you for enabling the publication of this third book.

And finally, thank you to the men and women of great achievement who have shared their many words of wisdom and experience. Without their insights, this book could never be possible.

Thank you.

Accountability

1. "The best preparation for the future is the present well seen to, and the last duty done."

George Macdonald (Author & Poet)

2. "I don't think of myself as a poor deprived ghetto girl who made good. I think of myself as somebody who from an early age knew I was responsible for myself, and I had to make good."

Oprah Winfrey (Talk Show Host & Media Mogul)

3. "No snowflake in an avalanche ever feels responsible."

Stanislaus Leszczynski (18th Century Polish King)

4. "It is wrong and immoral to seek to escape the consequences of one's acts."

Mahatma Gandhi (Civil Rights Leader & Activist)

5. "The happiest people in the world are those who feel absolutely terrific about themselves, and this is the natural outgrowth of accepting total responsibility for every part of their life."

Brian Tracy (Entrepreneur & Speaker)

Action

6. "We are always complaining that our days are few, and then acting as though there would be no end to them."

Seneca (Roman Philosopher & Statesman)

7. "'Freedom' and 'love' are simple words. They are not simple actions."

M. Scott Peck (Psychiatrist & Author)

8. "The way to get started is to quit talking and begin doing."

Walt Disney (Entertainment Entrepreneur)

9. "You can't build a reputation on what you're going to do."

Henry Ford (Industrialist)

10. "Knowing is not enough; we must apply. Wishing is not enough; we must do."

Johann Wolfgang von Goethe (German Writer & Statesman)

11. "The way to be nothing is to do nothing."

Nathaniel Howe (Early American Minister)

12. "What is it that makes men suppose that they can more easily do twice tomorrow what they didn't do once today?"

Richard L. Evans (Clergyman & Writer)

13. "The darkest day in life is the one in which we expect something for nothing."

Allen Shawn (Composer & Educator)

Adversity

14. "Don't let life discourage you: Everyone who got where he is had to begin where he was."

Richard L. Evans (Clergyman & Writer)

15. "Difficulties in life are intended to make us better not bitter."

Dan Reeves (American Football Coach & Former Player)

16. "All great and honorable actions are accompanied with great difficulties."

William Bradford (Early American Pilgrim Leader)

17. "Let me embrace thee, sour adversity, for wise men say it is the wisest course."

William Shakespeare (English Poet & Playwright)

18. "Comfort and prosperity have never enriched the world as much as adversity has."

Billy Graham (Minister)

Ambition

19. "Absence of occupation is not rest; a mind quite vacant is a mind distressed."

William Cowper (18th Century English Poet)

20. "To be happy at home is the ultimate result of all ambition."

Samuel Johnson (18th Century Writer & Poet)

21. "The tragedy of life is not that it ends so soon, but that we wait so long to begin it."

Richard L. Evans (Clergyman & Writer)

22. "Intelligence without ambition is a bird without wings."

Salvadore Dali (Artist)

Attitude

23. "The real winners in life are the people who look at every situation with an expectation that they can make it work or make it better."

Barbara Pletcher (20th Century American Writer)

24. "Attitude is a little thing that makes a big difference."

Winston Churchill (British Statesman, Prime Minister & Writer)

25. "Think you can, think you can't; either way, you'll be right."

Henry Ford (Industrialist)

26. "A cloudy day is no match for a sunny disposition."

William Arthur Ward (Writer & Education Administrator)

27. "Life is 10 percent what you make it, and 90 percent how you take it."

Irving Berlin (20th Century Songwriter)

Authority

28. "Those who have been given a little authority begin to think what they could do with a little more authority."

Richard L. Evans (Clergyman & Writer)

29. "Nothing strengthens authority so much as silence."

Leonardo da Vinci (Italian Artist & Inventor)

30. "Moral authority comes from following universal and timeless principles like honesty, integrity, treating people with respect."

Stephen R. Covey (Educator & Author)

31. "Those who enjoy responsibility usually get it; those who merely like exercising authority usually lose it."

Malcolm Forbes (Publisher)

Change

32. "Change always comes bearing gifts."

Price Pritchett (Writer & Business Consultant)

33. "Change before you have to."

Jack Welch (Business Executive)

34. "An obstinate man does not hold opinions - they hold him."

Samuel Butler (19th Century English Writer)

35. "There is a difference between being convinced and being stubborn. I'm not certain what the difference is, but I do know that if you butt your head against a stone wall long enough, at some point you realize the wall is stone and that your head is flesh and blood."

Maya Angelou (Poet & Author)

36. "The only real security in life lies in relishing life's insecurity."

M. Scott Peck (Psychiatrist & Author)

Character

37. "A man's character is like a tree, and his reputation like its shadow; the shadow is what we think of it; the tree is the real thing."

Abraham Lincoln (U.S. President)

38. "Habits change into character."

Ovid (Roman Poet)

39. "Talent without character, beauty, money, power, influence, eloquence - anything without character - is a hazard and a cause of concern. Character will always be found the best safeguard of virtue - and of all else that makes life safe and satisfying."

Richard L. Evans (Clergyman & Writer)

40. "Character is what you are in the dark."

Dwight L. Moody (19th Century American Minister & Publisher)

41. "The future is something which everyone reaches at the rate of sixty minutes an hour, whatever he does, whoever he is."

C.S. Lewis (Novelist)

Commitment

42. "Faithless is he that says farewell when the road darkens."

J.R.R. Tolkien (Writer & Professor)

43. "When you're surrounded by people who share a passionate commitment to a common purpose, anything is possible."

Howard Schultz (American Business Executive)

44. "The quality of a person's life is in direct proportion to their commitment to excellence, regardless of their chosen field of endeavor."

Vince Lombardi (American Football Coach)

45. "You always have two choices: your commitment versus your fear."

Sammy Davis, Jr. (Entertainer)

Communication

46. "The ability to deal with people is as purchasable a commodity as sugar or coffee, and I will pay more for that ability than for any other under the sun."

John D. Rockefeller (Industrialist)

47. "The real art of conversation is not only to say the right thing at the right place but to leave unsaid the wrong thing at the tempting moment."

Dorothy Nevill (Horticulturist)

48. "Courage is what it takes to stand up and speak. Courage is also what it takes to sit down and listen."

Winston Churchill (British Statesman, Prime Minister & Writer)

49. "The ability to communicate with everybody, regardless of who are you are, is a great thing."

Bobby Bonilla (American Baseball Player)

50. "There is, indeed, no wild beast more to be dreaded than a communicative man having nothing to communicate."

Jonathan Swift (Irish Poet)

51. "To know oneself is to study oneself in action with another person."

Bruce Lee (Martial Artist & Philosopher)

52. "The art of conversation is to be prompt without being stubborn, to refute without argument, and to clothe great matters in a motley garb."

Benjamin Disraeli (19th Century British Prime Minister)

53. "It is not he who gains the exact point in dispute who scores most in controversy - but he who has shown the better temper."

Samuel Butler (19th Century English Writer)

54. "Perhaps you will forget tomorrow the kind words you say today, but the recipient may cherish them over a lifetime."

Dale Carnegie (American Author & Speaker)

55. "Wise men talk because they have something to say; fools, because they have to say something."

Plato (Greek Philosopher)

Confidence

56. "While it is wise to accept what we cannot change about ourselves, it is also good to remember that we are never too old to replace discouragement with bits and pieces of confidence and hope."

Elaine N. Aron (Psychotherapist)

57. "Self trust is the first secret of success."

Ralph Waldo Emerson (19th Century American Writer)

58. "Confidence is contagious. So is lack of confidence."

Vince Lombardi (American Football Coach)

59. "A man's doubts and fears are his worst enemies. "

William Wrigley Jr. (19th Century Businessman)

Conquering Fear

60. "If anything terrifies me, I must try to conquer it."

Francis Chichester (Aviator & Sailor)

61. "I learned that courage was not the absence of fear, but the triumph over it. The brave man is not he who does not feel afraid, but he who conquers that fear."

Nelson Mandela (Former President of South Africa)

62. "Inaction breeds doubt and fear. Action breeds confidence and courage. If you want to conquer fear, do not sit home and think about it. Go out and get busy."

Dale Carnegie (American Author & Speaker)

63. "There is no terror in a bang, only in anticipation of it."

Alfred Hitchcock (Filmmaker)

64. "There is no greater hell than to be a prisoner of fear."

Ben Jonson (English Playwright)

Courage

65. "Courage doesn't mean you don't get afraid. Courage means you don't let fear stop you."

Bethany Hamilton (Professional Surfing Champion)

66. "Tell a person they are brave and you help them become so."

Thomas Carlyle (Scottish Philosopher & Writer)

67. "Only when we are no longer afraid do we begin to live."

Dorothy Thompson (Journalist & Radio Broadcaster)

68. "Courage is doing what you're afraid to do. There can be no courage unless you're scared."

Edward Vernon Rickenbacker (American World War I Fighter Pilot)

69. "Perhaps everything terrible is, in its deepest being, something helpless that wants help from us."

Rainer Maria Rilke (Austrian Poet & Novelist)

70. "Bravery never goes out of fashion."

William Makepeace Thackeray (19th Century English Novelist)

71. "Without courage, all other virtues lose their meaning."

Winston Churchill (British Statesman, Prime Minister & Writer)

72. "Courage is the greatest of all the virtues, because if you haven't courage, you may not have an opportunity to use any of the others."

Samuel Johnson (18th Century Writer & Poet)

73. "Courage is the most of all the virtues. Because without courage you cannot practice any other virtue consistently. You can be anything erratically. Kind, true, generous, fair, merciful, just, any of those things occasionally. But to be that thing time after time demands that you have courage."

Maya Angelou (Poet & Author)

74. "Courage is grace under pressure."

Ernest Hemingway (American Novelist & Journalist)

Creativity

75. "Whatever creativity is, it is in part a solution to a problem."

Brian Aldiss (British Fiction Writer)

76. "Nobody talks of entrepreneurship as survival, but that's exactly what it is and what nurtures creative thinking."

Anita Roddick (Entrepreneur)

77. "A major stimulant to creative thinking is focused questions. There is something about a well-worded question that often penetrates to the heart of the matter and triggers new ideas and insights."

Brian Tracy (Entrepreneur & Speaker)

78. "Creativity and innovation are something you can't flowchart out... A lot of companies have innovation departments, and this is always a sign that something is wrong."

Tim Cook (Business Executive)

79. "He who works with his hands is a laborer; he who works with his hand and his head is an artisan; he who works with his hand and his head and his heart is an artist."

T.V. Smith (English Musician)

80. "A hunch is creativity trying to tell you something."

Frank Capra (Film Director)

81. "We all die. The goal isn't to live forever, the goal is to create something that will."

Chuck Palahniuk (American Author)

82. "If you want to have good ideas, you must have many ideas. Most of them will be wrong, and what you have to learn is which ones to throw away."

Linus Pauling (Chemist)

83. "When inspiration touches talent, she gives birth to truth and beauty."

Steven   Pressfield   (Novelist   & Screenwriter)

84. "Discovery consists of seeing what everybody has seen and thinking what nobody has thought."

Albert Szent-Gyorgyi (Hungarian Physiologist)

85. "To live a creative life, we must lose our fear of being wrong."

Joseph Chilton Pearce (Child Development Expert & Writer)

86. "I don't play the same notes each time, I play the song, and the song plays me. We are the same."

Willie Nelson (American Musician)

87. "Imagination is more important than knowledge."

Albert Einstein (German Physicist)

Dealing with Failure

88. "In times of great stress or adversity, it's always best to keep busy, to plow your anger and your energy into something positive."

Lee Iacocca (Business Executive)

89. "Experience is what you get when you didn't get what you wanted."

Randy Pausch (American Professor & Lecturer)

90. "Always look at what you have left. Never look at what you have lost."

Robert Schuller (Minister)

91. "Success is a lousy teacher. It seduces smart people into thinking they can't lose."

Bill Gates (Inventor & Entrepreneur)

92. "It is not fun to fail. But it can be highly educational...We probably have even more to learn from our failures than from our successes."

M. Scott Peck (Psychiatrist & Author)

93. "The world breaks everyone, and afterward, some are stronger at the broken places."

Ernest Hemingway (American Novelist & Journalist)

94. "The indispensable first step to getting the things you want out of life is this: decide what you want."

Ben Stein (American Lawyer & Actor)

95. "We must learn not to let the fear of failure make us fail, and not to let our fears make our failures final."

Richard L. Evans (Clergyman & Writer)

96. "You may not realize it when it happens, but a kick in the teeth may be the best thing in the world for you."

Walt Disney (Entertainment Entrepreneur)

97. "To make no mistakes is not in the power of man; but from their errors and mistakes, the wise and the good learn wisdom for the future."

Plutarch (Greek Historian & Writer)

Decision-Making

98. "Remembering that I'll be dead soon is the most important tool I've ever encountered to help me make the big choices in life. Because almost everything - all external expectations, all pride, all fear of embarrassment or failure - these things just fall away in the face of death, leaving only what is truly important. Remembering that you are going to die is the best way I know to avoid the trap of thinking you have something to lose. You are already naked. There is no reason not to follow your heart."

Steve Jobs (Entrepreneur)

99. "One of the marks of the executive is the ability to decide. One of the obligations of free men is the willingness to decide. One of the qualities of effective people is the courage to decide."

Richard L. Evans (Clergyman & Writer)

100. "Decisiveness is a characteristic of high-performing men and women. Almost any decision is better than no decision at all."

Brian Tracy (Entrepreneur & Speaker)

101. "The best decision-makers are those who are willing to suffer the most over their decisions but still retain their ability to be decisive."

M. Scott Peck (Psychiatrist & Author)

Determination

102. "Nothing splendid has ever been achieved except by those who dared believe that something inside them was superior to circumstance."

Bruce Barton (American Politician & Businessman)

103. "You can never quit. Winners never quit, and quitters never win."

Ted Turner (Media Mogul)

104. "The only difference between successful people and unsuccessful people is extraordinary determination."

Mary Kay Ash (American Entrepreneur)

105. "The first rule is to keep an untroubled spirit. The second is to look things in the face and know them for what they are."

Marcus Aurelius (Roman Emperor)

106. "Age wrinkles the body. Quitting wrinkles the soul."

Douglas MacArthur (U.S. Army General)

107. "Never give in! Never give in! Never, never, never. Never - in anything great or small, large or petty - never give in except to convictions of honor and good sense."

Winston Churchill (British Statesman, Prime Minister & Writer)

108. "Don't live down to expectations. Go out there and do something remarkable."

Wendy Wasserstein (American Playwright)

109. "Let every man sing his own song in life."

John A. Widtsoe (Clergyman)

Discipline

110. "No man is free who is not master of himself."

Epictetus (Greek Philosopher)

111. "I have never known a really successful man who deep in his heart did not understand the grind, the discipline it takes to win."

Vince Lombardi (American Football Coach)

112. "You can enhance the pleasure of life by meeting and experiencing the pain first and getting it over with."

M. Scott Peck (Psychiatrist & Author)

113. "A disciplined conscience is a man's best friend."

Austin Phelps (19th Century Minister)

114. "It must be the aim of education to teach the citizen that he must first of all rule himself."

Winthrop A. Aldrich (American Business Executive)

115. "I am a great believer in luck, and I find that the harder I work, the more I have of it."

Thomas Jefferson (U.S. President)

116. "Practice isn't the thing you do once you're good. It's the thing you do that makes you good."

Malcolm Gladwell (Writer)

117. "Patience serves as a protection against wrongs as clothes do against cold. For if you put on more clothes as the cold increases, it will have no power to hurt you."

Leonardo da Vinci (Italian Artist & Inventor)

118. "Prove that you can control yourself and you are an educated man; and without this all other education is good for nothing."

Roswell Dwight Hitchcock (19th Century Clergyman)

119. "The greatest remedy for anger is delay."

Seneca (Roman Philosopher & Statesman)

Dreams

120. "All men who have achieved great things have been great dreamers."

Orison Swett Marden (American Author & Publisher)

121. "Every great dream begins with a dreamer. Always remember, you have within you the strength, the patience and the passion to reach for the stars to change the world."

Harriet Tubman (19th Century American Abolitionist)

122. "If you can dream it, you can do it."

Walt Disney (Entertainment Entrepreneur)

123. "Every man dies. Not every man lives. The only limits to possibilities in your life tomorrow are the 'buts' you use today."

Les Brown (American Speaker)

124. "It's important to have specific dreams."

Randy Pausch (American Professor & Lecturer)

Education

125. "The only real security that a man will have in this world is a reserve of knowledge, experience and ability."

Henry Ford (Industrialist)

126. "It is the studying that you do after your school days that really counts. Otherwise, you know only that which everyone else knows."

Henry Doherty (Entrepreneur)

127. "Education is for improving the lives of others and for leaving your community and world better than you found it."

Marian Wright Edelman (American Activist & Attorney)

128. "My grandmother used to tell me that a hard head makes a sore ass."

Willie Nelson (American Musician)

129. "If we could sell our experiences for what they cost us, we'd all be millionaires."

Abigail Van Buren (Advice Columnist)

130. "Learning without thought is labor lost; thought without learning is perilous."

Confucius (Chinese Philosopher)

131. "Of all the diversions of life, there is none so proper to fill up its empty spaces as the reading of useful and entertaining authors."

Joseph Addison (English Playwright)

132. "If a nation expects to be ignorant and free, in a state of civilization, it expects what never was and never will be."

Thomas Jefferson (U.S. President)

133. "Relinquish rigid ideas about who you are, and challenge yourself with new experiences and new perspectives."

Deepak Chopra (Author & Physician)

134. "A man learns to skate by staggering about making a fool of himself; indeed, he progresses in all things by making a fool of himself."

George Bernard Shaw (Irish Playwright)

135. "What we actually learn, from any given set of circumstances, determines whether we become increasingly powerless or more powerful."

Blaine Lee (American Entrepreneur)

136. "We know the truth, not only by the reason, but also by the heart."

Blaise Pascal (French Mathematician & Inventor)

137. "Much reading is like much eating - wholly useless without digestion."

Robert South (British Clergyman)

138. "He that is taught only by himself has a fool for a master."

Ben Jonson (English Playwright)

139. "For I do not seek to understand in order to believe, but I believe in order to understand.   For I believe this: unless I believe, I will not understand."

Anselm of Canterbury (11th Century Philosopher & Writer)

140. "Education is a progressive discovery of our own ignorance."

Will Durant (Writer & Historian)

141. "Education makes a people easy to lead, but difficult to drive; easy to govern, but impossible to enslave."

Henry Peter Brougham (British Statesman)

142. "If the world learned from history, how different would both be."

Arnold Glasow (20th Century American Writer)

143. "Some books are to be tasted, others to be swallowed, and some few to be chewed and digested."

Francis Bacon (English Writer & Scientist)

144. "History is a guide to navigation in perilous times. History is who we are and why we are the way we are."

David McCullough (Writer & Historian)

145. "An organization's ability to learn, and translate that learning into action rapidly, is the ultimate competitive business advantage."

Jack Welch (Business Executive)

146. "The deadliest foe to virtue would be complete self-knowledge."

Francis Herbert Bradley (British Philosopher)

Enthusiasm

147. "We act as though comfort and luxury were the chief requirements of life, when all we need to make us really happy is something to be enthusiastic about."

Charles Kingsley (Novelist & Professor)

148. "Life is fragile. We're not guaranteed a tomorrow so give it everything you've got."

Tim Cook (Business Executive)

149. "Life is a great big canvas, and you should throw all the paint you can on it."

Danny Kaye (Actor & Singer)

150. "What is passion? It is surely the becoming of a person."

John Boorman (Irish Filmmaker)

151. "Those who wish to sing always find a song."

Swedish Proverb

152. "A man without a passion is like a vessel waiting for wind and not budging."

Arsene Houssaye (French Novelist & Poet)

153. "We don't stop playing because we grow old; we grow old because we stop playing."

George Bernard Shaw (Irish Playwright)

154. "Don't be afraid of death so much as an inadequate life."

Bertolt Brecht (German Playwright & Poet)

155. "Only passions, great passions, can elevate the soul to great things."

Denis Diderot (18th Century French Philosopher & Writer)

156. "We act as though comfort and luxury were the chief requirements of life, when all we need to make us really happy is something to be enthusiastic about."

Charles Kingsley (19th Century English Historian & Writer)

Entrepreneurship

157. "Everyone starts from scratch, but not everyone keeps on scratching!"

Author Unknown

158. "Three components make an entrepreneur: the person, the idea, and the resources to make it happen."

Anita Roddick (Entrepreneur)

159. "If you don't drive your business, you will be driven out of business."

B.C. Forbes (Writer & Publisher)

160. "The only way to do great work is to love what you do."

Steve Jobs (Entrepreneur)

161. "A market is never saturated with a good product, but it is very quickly saturated with a bad one."

Henry Ford (Industrialist)

Ethics

162. "To see what is right and not do it is a lack of courage."

Confucius (Chinese Philosopher)

163. "What is right to be done cannot be done too soon."

Jane Austen (English Novelist)

164. "If we do not maintain Justice,

Justice will not maintain us."

Francis Bacon (English Writer & Scientist)

165. "I am not a product of my circumstances. I am a product of my decisions."

Stephen R. Covey (Educator & Author)

Focus

166. "When you're riding, only the race in which you're riding is important."

Bill Shoemaker (Jockey)

167. "I skate to where the puck is going to be, not where it has been."

Wayne Gretzky (Hockey Player & Coach)

168. "Who begins too much accomplishes little."

German Proverb

169. "Concentration can be cultivated. One can learn to exercise will power, discipline one's body and train one's mind."

Anil Ambani (Indian Business Executive & Philanthropist)

170. "The man who chases two rabbits catches neither."

Confucius (Chinese Philosopher)

171. "You can only do so many things great, and you should cast aside everything else."

Tim Cook (Business Executive)

Goal Setting

172. "Dreams never hurt anybody if you keep working right behind the dreams to make as much of them become real as you can."

Frank Woolworth (American Entrepreneur)

173. "If you do not think about your future, you cannot have one."

John Galsworthy (English Novelist & Playwright)

174. "The greater danger for most of us lies not in setting our aim too high and falling short, but in setting our aim too low and achieving our mark."

Michelangelo (Italian Artist)

175. "A good goal is like a strenuous exercise - it makes you stretch."

Mary Kay Ash (American Entrepreneur)

176. "A successful individual typically sets his next goal somewhat but not too much above his last achievement. In this way he steadily raises his level of aspiration."

Kurt Lewin (Psychologist)

177. "If one advances confidently in the direction of his dreams, and endeavors to live the life he has imagined, he will meet with a success unexpected in common hours."

Henry David Thoreau (19th Century American Writer & Philosopher)

178. "Any person who selects a goal in life which can be fully achieved, has already defined his own limitations."

Cavett Robert (American Entrepreneur & Public Speaker)

179. "You are never too old to set another goal or to dream a new dream."

C.S. Lewis (Novelist)

180. "If you want to achieve a high goal, you're going to have to take some chances."

Alberto Salazar (American Athlete & Coach)

181. "You need to overcome the tug of people against you as you reach for high goals."

George S. Patton (U.S. Army General)

182. "Vision without action is a daydream. Action without vision is a nightmare."

Japanese Proverb

183. "Always dream and shoot higher than you know you can do. Don't bother just to be better than your contemporaries or predecessors. Try to be better than yourself."

William Faulkner (American Writer)

Habits

184. "The chains of habit are generally too small to be felt until they are too strong to be broken."

Samuel Johnson (18th Century Writer & Poet)

185. "We first make our habits, and then our habits make us."

John Dryden (17th Century English Poet & Playwright)

186. "The habits of time are the soul's dress for eternity."

George B. Cheever (American Clergyman)

187. "We are what we repeatedly do."

Aristotle (Greek Philosopher)

Ideas

188. "Ideas are a dime a dozen. People who implement them are priceless."

Mary Kay Ash (American Entrepreneur)

189. "Ideas are like rabbits. You get a couple and learn how to handle them, and pretty soon you have a dozen."

John Steinbeck (American Author)

190. "Ideas must work through the brains and the arms of good and brave men, or they are no better than dreams."

Ralph Waldo Emerson (19th Century American Writer)

191. "The unreal is more powerful than the real, because nothing is as perfect as you can imagine it, because it's only intangible ideas, concepts beliefs, fantasies that last. Stone crumbles, wood rots. People, well, they die. But things as fragile as a thought, a dream, a legend, they can go on and on."

Chuck Palahniuk (Novelist)

Imagination

192. "You can't do it unless you can imagine it."

George Lucas (Film Director)

193. "A strong imagination begetteth opportunity."

Michel de Montaigne (16th Century French Philosopher)

194. "Live out of your imagination, not your history."

Stephen R. Covey (Educator & Writer)

195. "Your imagination is your preview of life's coming attractions."

Albert Einstein (German Physicist)

Innovation

196. "Sometimes when you innovate, you make mistakes. It is best to admit them quickly and get on with improving your other innovations."

Steve Jobs (Entrepreneur)

197. "The reasonable man adapts himself to the world; the unreasonable one persists in trying to adapt the world to himself. Therefore all progress depends on the unreasonable man."

George Bernard Shaw (Irish Playwright)

198. "The best way to predict the future is to invent it."

Alan Kay (Entrepreneur & Researcher)

199. "Genius is one percent inspiration and ninety-nine percent perspiration."

Thomas Edison (Inventor & Businessman)

Integrity

200. "We have all had the experience of finding that our reactions and perhaps even our deeds have denied beliefs we thought were ours."

James Baldwin (Novelist & Playwright)

201. "We lie loudest when we lie to ourselves."

Eric Hoffer (American Writer & Philosopher)

202. "The only immorality is not to do what one has to do when one has to do it."

Jean Anouilh (French Playwright)

203. "To be nobody but yourself in a world which is doing its best night and day to make you like everybody else means to fight the hardest battle any human being can fight and never stop fighting."

E.E. Cummings (American Writer)

204. "Conscience is a divine voice in the human soul."

Francis Bowen (19th Century American Philosopher & Writer)

205. "I think there is only one quality worse than hardness of heart, and that is softness of head."

Theodore Roosevelt (U.S. President)

206. "A quiet conscience makes one strong!"

Anne Frank (German Diarist & Writer)

Knowledge

207. "A man is but what he knoweth."

Francis Bacon (English Writer & Scientist)

208. "The worth of a book is to be measured by what you can carry away from it."

James Bryce (British Historian & Statesman)

209. "The man who does not read good books has no advantage over the man who can't read them."

Mark Twain (American Writer)

210. "Knowledge is indivisible. When people grow wise in one direction, they are sure to make it easier for themselves to grow wise in other directions as well."

Isaac Asimov (Writer & Professor)

211. "Surprise drives progress because innovation depends on the sort of knowledge no one can gather in a central place."

Virginia Postrel (Writer)

Leadership

212. "Who has not served cannot command."

John Florio (Italian Writer & Lexicographer)

213. "The man who questions opinion is wise; the man who quarrels with fact is a fool."

Frank A. Garbutt (Entrepreneur)

214. "If your actions inspire others to dream more, learn more, do more and become more, you are a leader."

John Quincy Adams (U.S. President)

215. "Leadership consists of nothing but taking responsibility for everything that goes wrong and giving your subordinates credit for everything that goes well."

Dwight D. Eisenhower (U.S. President)

216. "Strong beliefs win strong men, and then make them stronger."

Walter Bagehot (19th Century British Journalist)

217. "Tell me and I'll forget. Show me and I'll remember. Involve me and I'll understand."

Confucius (Chinese Philosopher)

218. "Leadership is action, not position."

Donald H. McGannon (American Broadcaster)

219. "You can motivate by fear, and you can motivate by reward. But both those methods are only temporary. The only lasting thing is self motivation."

Homer Rice (American Football Player & Coach)

220. "When you're in your nineties and looking back, it's not going to be how many awards you've won. It's really what did you stand for. Did you make a positive difference for people?"

Elizabeth Dole (American Politician)

221. "Flexibility in a time of great change is a vital quality of leadership."

Brian Tracy (Entrepreneur & Speaker)

222. "Anyone can hold the helm when the sea is calm."

Publilius Syrus (Roman Playwright)

Listening

223. "It takes a great man to be a good listener."

Calvin Coolidge (US President)

224. "Most of the successful people I've known are the ones who do more listening than talking."

Bernard Baruch (American Businessman & Statesman)

225. "Most people do not listen with the intent to understand; they listen with the intent to reply."

Stephen R. Covey (Educator & Author)

226. "The art of conversation lies in listening."

Malcolm Forbes (Publisher)

Luck

227. "I've found that luck is quite predictable. If you want more luck, take more chances. Be more active. Show up more often."

Brian Tracy (Entrepreneur & Speaker)

228. "Shallow men believe in luck. Strong men believe in cause and effect."

Ralph Waldo Emerson (19th Century American Writer)

229. "I think luck is the sense to recognize an opportunity and the ability to take advantage of it. The man who can smile at his breaks and grab his chances gets on."

Samuel Goldwyn (Entertainment Entrepreneur)

230. "Diligence is the mother of good luck."

Benjamin Franklin (American Statesman & Inventor)

231. "Luck is a matter of preparation meeting opportunity."

Seneca (Roman Philosopher & Statesman)

232. "The best luck is the luck you make for yourself."

Douglas MacArthur (U.S. Army General)

Management

233. "The one word that makes a good manager - decisiveness."

Lee Iacocca (American Business Executive)

234. "Too many people overvalue what they are not and undervalue what they are."

Malcolm Forbes (Publisher)

235. "A decision is the action an executive must take when he has information so incomplete that the answer does not suggest itself."

Arthur Radford (U.S. Navy Admiral)

236. "It doesn't make sense to hire smart people and tell them what to do; we hire smart people so they can tell us what to do."

Steve Jobs (Entrepreneur)

Motivation

237. "You simply have to put one foot in front of the other and keep going. Put blinders on and plow right ahead."

George Lucas (Film Director)

238. "Sometimes we feel that we've got to climb a mountain or raise a monument to leave our mark on the world. What we fail to recognize is that often we make a difference simply by existing, by handling what life gives us. Maybe the way we deal with our challenges and our rewards inspires someone else to achieve worthwhile things in their own life."

Blaine Lee (American Entrepreneur)

239. "Here is the test to find whether your mission on Earth is finished: If you're alive, it isn't."

Richard Bach (American Writer)

240. "Our greatest enemies, the ones we must fight most often, are within."

Thomas Paine (18th Century American Political Activist)

241. "Life begins when you do."

Hugh Downs (American Broadcaster)

242. "Peace of mind as our single goal is the most potent motivating force we can have."

Gerald Jampolsky (American Writer & Physician)

243. "People who are unable to motivate themselves must be content with mediocrity."

Andrew Carnegie (Scottish-American Industrialist)

244. "The most powerful weapon on earth is the human soul on fire."

Ferdinand Foch (French Military Leader)

245. "Viewed narrowly, all life is universal hunger and an expression of energy associated with it."

Mary Ritter Beard (American Historian & Activist)

246. "The big question is whether you are going to be able to say a hearty yes to your adventure."

Joseph Campbell (Writer & Philosopher)

Opportunity

247. "Opportunity is missed by most people because it is dressed in overalls and looks like work."

Thomas Edison (Inventor & Businessman)

248. "In the middle of difficulty lies opportunity."

Albert Einstein (German Physicist)

249. "When you innovate, you've got to be prepared for everyone telling you you're nuts."

Larry Ellison (Entrepreneur)

250. "There is a time to let things happen and a time to make things happen."

Hugh Prather (Writer & Minister)

251. "Everyone has talent. What is rare is the courage to follow the talent to the dark place where it leads."

Erica Jong (Author)

252. "One of the greatest pains to human nature is the pain of a new idea."

Walter Bagehot (19th Century British Journalist)

253. "A wise man will make more opportunities than he finds."

Francis Bacon (English Writer & Scientist)

254. "What is opportunity to the man who can't use it?"

George Eliot (19th Century English Novelist)

Overcoming Obstacles

255. "Now, here you see, it takes all the running you can do, to keep in the same place. If you want to get somewhere else, you must run at least twice as fast as that!"

Lewis Carroll (19th Century Mathematician & Writer)

256. "No man knows how much he can endure until he must. Strength, patience, and ability increase with necessity."

Richard L. Evans (Clergyman & Writer)

257. "Success is to be measured not so much by the position that one has reached in life as by the obstacles which he has overcome."

Booker T. Washington (American Educator & Author)

258. "Trouble shared is trouble halved."

Lee Iacocca (Business Executive)

259. "When you do the work to clearly identify and understand what your life's mission is all about and what your aim is, it can act as a beacon - a light that guides your everyday decisions such as what to do with your time, energy, and abilities. That focal point can become a source of resilience."

Bill Phillips (Fitness Writer & Publisher)

260. "Only those who dare to fail greatly can ever achieve greatly."

John F. Kennedy (U.S. President)

261. "When I was young, I observed that nine out of 10 things I did were failures, so I did 10 times more work."

George Bernard Shaw (Irish Playwright)

262. "Real life isn't always going to be perfect or go our way, but the recurring acknowledgement of what is working in our lives can help us not only survive but surmount our difficulties."

Sarah Ban Breathnach (Writer)

263. "Keep your fears to yourself, but share your inspiration with others."

Robert Louis Stevenson (Scottish Novelist)

264. "A man can get discouraged many times, but he is not a failure until he begins to blame somebody else and stops trying."

John Burroughs (American Conservationist)

265. "We could never learn to be brave and patient, if there were only joy in the world."

Helen Keller (Author & Activist)

266. "The fiery trials through which we pass will light us down in honor or dishonor to the latest generation."

Abraham Lincoln (U.S. President)

267. "Humor is the instinct for taking pain playfully."

Max Eastman (Writer & Poet)

268. "Who will tell whether one happy moment of love, or the joy of breathing or walking on a bright morning and smelling the fresh air, is not worth all the suffering and effort which life implies?"

Erich Fromm (German Psychologist)

269. "The truth is that many people never understand, until it is too late, is that the more you try to avoid suffering the more you suffer because smaller and more insignificant things begin to torture you in proportion to your fear of being hurt."

Thomas Merton (Poet & Monk)

270. "Life is a grindstone, and whether it grinds you down or polishes you up is for you and you alone to decide."

Cavett Robert (American Entrepreneur & Public Speaker)

271. "If you're not making mistakes, you're not trying hard enough."

Vince Lombardi (American Football Coach)

272. "No man's error becomes his own Law; nor obliges him to persist in it."

Thomas Hobbes (English Philosopher)

Perseverance

273. "He conquers who endures."

Persius (Roman Poet)

274. "Let perseverance be your engine, and hope your fuel."

H. Jackson Brown, Jr. (Writer)

275. "Endure, and keep yourselves for days of happiness."

Virgil (Roman Poet)

276. "Big shots are only little shots who keep shooting."

Christopher Morley (American Writer)

277. "Life is not so much about beginnings and endings as it is about going on and on. It is about muddling through the middle."

Anna Quindlen (Journalist & Novelist)

278. "The difference in winning and losing is most often, not quitting."

Walt Disney (Entertainment Entrepreneur)

279. "It does not matter how slowly you go up, so long as you don't stop."

Confucius (Chinese Philosopher)

280. "A hero is an ordinary individual who finds the strength to persevere and endure in spite of overwhelming obstacles."

Christopher Reeve (Actor)

Persistence

281. "We are made to persist. That's how we find out who we are."

Tobias Wolff (Author)

282. "I fear not the man who has practiced 10 000 kicks once, but I fear the man who has practiced one kick 10 000 times."

Bruce Lee (Martial Artist & Philosopher)

283. "When nothing seems to help, I go and look at a stonecutter hammering away at his rock perhaps a hundred times without as much as a crack showing in it. Yet at the hundred and first blow it will split in two, and I know it was not that blow that did it - but all that had gone before."

Jacob Riis (Journalist)

284. "A champion is one who gets up even when he can't."

Jack Dempsey (Boxer)

285. "It's not whether you get knocked down. It's whether you get up again."

Vince Lombardi (American Football Coach)

286. "The barriers are not erected which can say to aspiring talents and industry, 'Thus far and no farther.'"

Ludwig van Beethoven (German Composer)

287. "History never looks like history when you are living through it. It always looks confusing and messy, and it always feels uncomfortable."

John W. Gardener (U.S. Statesman)

288. "When you get into a tight place and everything goes against you till it seems you could not hold on a minute longer, never give up then, for that is just the place and time that the tide will turn."

Harriet Beecher Stowe (American Novelist & Abolitionist)

289. "Everyone starts from scratch, but not everyone keeps on scratching!"

Author Unknown

Planning

290. "If you only care enough for a result, you will almost certainly attain it."

William James (Philosopher & Psychologist)

291. "It takes as much energy to wish as it does to plan."

Eleanor Roosevelt (Politician & Activist)

292. "By failing to prepare, you are preparing to fail."

Benjamin Franklin (American Statesman & Inventor)

293. "Time is all you have. And you may find one day that you have less than you think."

Randy Pausch (American Professor & Lecturer)

294. "If you have accomplished all that you have planned for yourself, you have not planned enough."

Edward Everett Hale (Author & Minister)

295. "Plans are nothing. Planning is everything."

Dwight D. Eisenhower (U.S. President)

296. "Think ahead. Don't let day-to-day operations drive out planning."

Donald Rumsfeld (Statesman)

297. "Life is what happens while you're busy making other plans."

Allen Saunders (Writer)

298. "You can't plow a field simply by turning it over in your mind."

Gordon B. Hinckley (Minister)

299. "To succeed, planning alone is insufficient. One must improvise as well."

Isaac Asimov (Writer & Professor)

Positive Thinking

300. "I know of no more encouraging fact than the unquestionable ability of man to elevate his life by a conscious endeavor."

Henry David Thoreau (19th Century American Writer & Philosopher)

301. "What's the use of worrying?

It never was worth while,

So, pack up your troubles in your old kit-bag,

And smile, smile, smile."

George Asaf (Welsh Songwriter)

302. "Keep in mind that the words you use in your own self-talk can either be deflating and demoralizing or nurturing and reinforcing. It's vitally important that you recognize critical self-talk fast and replace it with something positive."

Bill Phillips (Fitness Writer & Publisher)

303. "Positive anything is better than negative thinking."

Elbert Hubbard (Writer & Publisher)

304. "Your own resolution to succeed is more important than any other one thing."

Abraham Lincoln (U.S. President)

305. "Change your thoughts and you change your world."

Norman Vincent Peale (Minister & Author)

306. "They are never alone that are accompanied with noble thoughts."

Sir Philip Sidney (16th Century Poet)

307. "I don't think anything is unrealistic if you believe you can do it."

Mike Ditka (American Football Coach)

308. "Only passions, great passions, can elevate the soul to great things."

Denis Diderot (18th Century French Philosopher & Writer)

309. "Keep a green tree in your heart and perhaps a singing bird will come."

Chinese Proverb

310. "Pressure is a word that is misused in our vocabulary. When you start thinking of pressure, it's because you've started to think of failure."

Tommy Lasorda (Baseball Player & Team Manager)

311. "If circumstances had the power to bless or harm, they would bless and harm all men alike, but the fact that the same circumstances will be alike good and bad to different souls proves that good or bad is not in the circumstance, but in the mind of him that encounters it."

James Allen (British Philosopher)

312. "There is no sadder sight than a young pessimist."

Mark Twain (American Writer)

313. "Without faith, nothing is possible. With it, nothing is impossible."

Mary Behune (Educator)

314. "Nature gave men two ends - one to sit on, and one to think with. Ever since then, man's success or failure has been dependent on the one he used the most."

George R. Kirkpatrick (Writer)

315. "Know how to live within yourself; there is in your soul a whole world of mysterious and enchanted thoughts; they will be drowned by the noise without; daylight will drive them away: listen to their singing and be silent."

Fyodor Tyutchev (Russian Poet)

316. "Nurture your mind with great thoughts. To believe in the heroic makes heroes."

Benjamin Disraeli (19th Century British Prime Minister)

317. "We either make ourselves miserable or we make ourselves strong. The amount of work is the same."

Carlos Castaneda (American Author)

318. "Sometimes the most proactive thing we can do is to just smile. Happiness, like unhappiness, is a proactive choice."

Stephen R. Covey (Educator & Author)

319. "Once you replace negative thoughts with positive ones, you'll start having positive results."

Willie Nelson (American Musician)

Preparation

320. "A winning effort begins with preparation."

Joe Gibbs (American Football Coach)

321. "There are no secrets to success. It is the result of preparation, hard work, and learning from failure."

Colin Powell (American Army General & Statesman)

322. "Dig the well before you are thirsty."

Chinese Proverb

323. "If I had eight hours to chop down a tree. I'd spend six sharpening my axe."

Abraham Lincoln (U.S. President)

324. "The future belongs to those who prepare for it."

Ralph Waldo Emerson (19th Century American Writer)

325. "The time to repair the roof is when the sun is shining."

John F. Kennedy (U.S. President)

326. "You don't rise to the occasion, you sink to the level of your training."

Author Unknown

Problem Solving

327. "It is a common experience that a problem difficult at night is resolved in the morning after the committee of sleep has worked on it."

John Steinbeck (American Author)

328. "Being smart is an elusive concept. There's a certain sharpness, an ability to absorb new facts, to ask an insightful question or relate to domains that may not seem connected at first."

Bill Gates (Inventor & Philanthropist)

329. "Each of us is a part of the problem or part of the answer."

Author Unknown

330. "The age-old axiom 'Sleep on it' is based in good science. The next time you need to solve a difficult problem or have a major life decision to make, give it the time and sleep it deserves."

Tom Rath (Author)

331. "You can solve any problem if you are simply willing to take the time."

M. Scott Peck (Psychiatrist & Author)

332. "Too many people go through life complaining about their problems. I've always believed that if you took one-tenth of the energy into complaining and applied it to solving the problem, you'd be surprised by how well things can work out."

Randy Pausch (American Professor & Lecturer)

333. "The problem is not that there are problems. The problem is expecting otherwise and thinking that having problems is a problem."

Theodore Rubin (Psychiatrist)

Progress

334. "Restlessness is discontent and discontent is the first necessity of progress."

Thomas Edison (Inventor & Businessman)

335. "The art of progress is to preserve order amid change and to preserve change amid order."

Alfred North Whitehead (English Mathematician & Philosopher)

336. "I was taught that the way of progress is neither swift nor easy."

Marie Curie (Polish Chemist)

337. "Coming together is a beginning; keeping together is progress; working together is success."

Henry Ford (Industrialist)

338. "Without continual growth and progress, such words as improvement, achievement, and success have no meaning."

Benjamin Franklin (American Statesman & Inventor)

339. "There are no constraints on the human mind, no walls around the human spirit, no barriers to our progress except those we ourselves erect."

Ronald Reagan (U.S. President)

340. "Develop an attitude of gratitude, and give thanks for everything that happens to you, knowing that every step forward is a step toward achieving something bigger and better than your current situation."

Brian Tracy (Entrepreneur & Speaker)

Purpose

341. "There comes a special moment in everyone's life; a moment for which that person was born. That special opportunity, when he seizes it, will fulfill his mission - a mission for which he is uniquely qualified. In that moment, he finds greatness. It is his finest hour."

Winston Churchill (British Statesman, Prime Minister & Writer)

342. "When everybody tells you that you are being idealistic or impractical, consider the possibility that everybody could be wrong about what is right for you."

Gilbert Kaplan (American Businessman & Publisher)

343. "Life well spent is long."

Leonardo da Vinci (Italian Artist & Inventor)

344. "Thank God every morning when you get up that you have something to do that day which must be done whether you like it or not."

Charles Kingsley (Novelist & Professor)

345. "A man can stand almost anything except a succession of ordinary days."

Johann Wolfgang von Goethe (German Writer & Statesman)

346. "Some men have thousands of reasons why they cannot do what they want to, when all they need is one reason why they can."

Willis R. Whitney (Chemist & Researcher)

347. "Great minds have purpose, others have wishes."

Washington Irving (Author & Historian)

348. "I've come to believe that each of us has a personal calling that's as unique as a fingerprint - and that the best way to succeed is to discover what you love and then find a way to offer it to others in the form of service, working hard, and also allowing the energy of the universe to lead you."

Oprah Winfrey (Talk Show Host & Media Mogul)

Responsibility

349. "Don't make excuses - make good."

Elbert Hubbard (Writer & Publisher)

350. "We must accept responsibility for a problem before we can solve it. We cannot solve a problem by saying 'It's not my problem,' and hope that someone else will solve it for us. We can solve a problem only when we say 'This is *my* problem and it's up to me to solve it.'"

M. Scott Peck (Psychiatrist & Author)

351. "The moment you truly decide to accept ownership of your health, happiness and life is the moment when everything begins to change. When you stop blaming others, give up the victim stories, and you accept responsibility, it's then and only then that you can harness your true power and ability to take control and make remarkable changes for the better."

Bill Phillips (Fitness Writer & Publisher)

352. "You cannot escape the responsibility of tomorrow by evading it today."

Abraham Lincoln (U.S. President)

353. "What is a fear of living? It's being preeminently afraid of dying. It is not doing what you came here to do, out of timidity and spinelessness. The antidote is to take full responsibility for yourself - for the time you take up and the space you occupy. If you don't know what you're here to do, then just do some good."

Maya Angelou (Poet & Author)

354. "Every right implies a responsibility; every opportunity, an obligation; every possession, a duty."

John D. Rockefeller (Industrialist)

355. "The price of greatness is responsibility."

Winston Churchill (British Statesman, Prime Minister & Writer)

356. "You are not only responsible for what you say, but also for what you do not say."

Martin Luther (German Theologian)

357. "Freedom means responsibility. That's why most men dread it."

George Bernard Shaw (Irish Playwright)

Results

358. "What impresses men is not mind, but the result of mind."

Walter Bagehot (19th Century British Journalist)

359. "I think one's feelings waste themselves in words; they ought all to be distilled into actions which bring results."

Florence Nightingale (English Social Activist & Nurse)

360. "However beautiful the strategy, you should occasionally look at the results."

Winston Churchill (British Statesman, Prime Minister & Writer)

361. "Miracles can be made, but only by sweating."

Giovanni Agnelli (Italian Industrialist & Businessman)

362. "Results! Why, man, I have gotten a lot of results. I know several thousand things that won't work."

Thomas Edison (Inventor & Businessman)

363. "Those who trust to chance must abide by the results of chance."

Calvin Coolidge (U.S. President)

Risk Taking

364. "He who is not courageous enough to take risks will accomplish nothing in life."

Muhammad Ali (Boxer)

365. "Only through curiosity can we discover opportunities, and only through gambling can we take advantage of them."

Clarence Birdseye (American Entrepreneur)

366. "If you want risk taking, set an example yourself and reward and praise those that do."

Jack Welch (Business Executive)

367. "If you take risks and face your fate with dignity, there is nothing you can do that makes you small; if you don't take risks, there is nothing you can do that makes you grand, nothing."

Nassim Nicholas Taleb (Lebanese Scientist & Philosopher)

368. "All life is a chance. The person who goes farthest is the one who is willing to do and dare."

Dale Carnegie (American Author & Speaker)

369. "If you don't fail now and again, it's a sign you're playing it safe."

Woody Allen (Film Director)

370. "Where the road bends abruptly, take short steps."

Ernest Bramah (English Author)

371. "Far better is it to dare mighty things, to win glorious triumphs, even though checkered by failure than to rank with those poor spirits who neither enjoy much nor suffer much, because they live in a gray twilight that knows not victory, nor defeat."

Theodore Roosevelt (U.S. President)

372. "There are risks and costs to a plan of action. But they are far less than the long-range risks and costs of comfortable inaction."

John F. Kennedy (U.S. President)

373. "Trust your own instinct. Your mistakes might as well be your own, instead of someone else's."

Billy Wilder (Film Director)

374. "I enjoy every opportunity and live every moment. And that is why I have no regrets. It's when you are not scared of losing that you win everything."

Shailendra Singh (Indian Singer)

Sacrifice

375. "You must do the things today that others will not do so that you can have the things tomorrow that others will not have."

Author Unknown

376. "Dreams do come true, if we only wish hard enough. You can have anything in life if you will sacrifice everything else for it."

J.M. Barrie (Scottish Author)

377. "Sacrifice is a part of life. It's supposed to be. It's not something to regret. It's something to aspire to."

Mitch Albom (Author & Media Personality)

378. "We now come to the grand law of the system in which we are placed, as it has been developed by the experience of our race, and that, in one word, is SACRIFICE!"

Catherine E. Beecher (American Educator)

379. "He who would accomplish little must sacrifice little; he who would achieve much must sacrifice much; he who would attain highly must sacrifice greatly."

James Allen (British Philosopher)

380. "Great achievement is usually born of great sacrifice, and is never the result of selfishness."

Napoleon Hill (Writer & Speaker)

Self-Control

381. "Anybody can become angry - that is easy; but to be angry with the right person, and to the right degree, and at the right time, and for the right purpose, and in the right way - that is not within everybody's power and that is not easy."

Aristotle (Greek Philosopher)

382. "When angry, count ten before you speak, if very angry, count a hundred."

Thomas Jefferson (U.S. President)

383. "The end of anger is sorrow."

Seneca (Roman Philosopher & Statesman)

384. "Anger is a wind which blows out the lamp of the mind."

Robert G. Ingersoll (19th Century American Activist)

385. "Industry, thrift and self-control are not sought because they create wealth, but because they create character."

Calvin Coolidge (U.S. President)

386. "Being forced to work, and forced to do your best, will breed in you temperance and self-control, diligence and strength of will, cheerfulness and content, and a hundred virtues which the idle will never know."

Charles Kingsley (Novelist & Professor)

387. "To enjoy good health, to bring true happiness to one's family, to bring peace to all, one must first discipline and control one's own mind. If a man can control his mind he can find the way to enlightenment, and all wisdom and virtue will naturally come to him."

Buddha (Philosopher & Teacher)

388. "There are two types of people: those who try to win and those who try to win arguments. They are never the same."

Nassim Nicholas Taleb (Lebanese Scientist & Philosopher)

Self Improvement

389. "The greatest use of life is to spend it for something that outlasts it."

William James (Philosopher & Psychologist)

390. "Be not merely good; be good for something."

Henry David Thoreau (19th Century American Writer & Philosopher)

391. "Look well into thyself; there is a source which will always spring up if thou wilt always search there."

Marcus Aurelius (Roman Emperor)

392. "When we are no longer able to change a situation, we are challenged to change ourselves."

Victor Frankl (Austrian Psychiatrist & Writer)

393. "Know how to listen, and you will profit even from those who talk badly."

Plutarch (Greek Historian & Writer)

394. "If you work long and hard enough to understand yourself, you will come to discover that your unconscious, a vast part of your mind of which you now have little awareness, contains riches beyond imagination."

M. Scott Peck (Psychiatrist & Author)

395. "First say to yourself what you would be; and then do what you have to do."

Epictetus (Greek Philosopher)

396. "Noble character is best appreciated in those ages in which it can most readily develop."

Tacitus (Roman Senator & Historian)

397. "You will become as small as your controlling desire; as great as your dominant aspiration."

James Allen (British Philosopher)

398. "Once in seven years I burn all my sermons; for it is a shame if I cannot write better sermons now than I did seven years ago."

John Wesley (18th Century Theologian & Minister)

399. "Make the most of yourself, for that is all there is of you."

Ralph Waldo Emerson (19th Century American Writer)

400. "You are the way you are because that's the way you want to be. If you really wanted to be any different, you would be in the process of changing right now."

Fred Smith (Entrepreneur & Business Executive)

401. "You get the best out of others when you get the best out of yourself."

Harvey Firestone (Businessman & Entrepreneur)

Selling

402. "Sales are contingent upon the attitude of the salesman - not the attitude of the prospect."

W. Clement Stone (Businessman & Writer)

403. "Pretend that every single person you meet has a sign around his or her neck that says, 'Make me feel important.' Not only will you succeed in sales, you will succeed in life."

Mary Kay Ash (American Entrepreneur)

404. "The fact is, everyone is in sales. Whatever area you work in, you do have clients and you do need to sell."

Jay Abraham (CEO & Marketing Executive)

405. "Samson killed a thousand men with the jaw bone of an ass. That many sales are killed every day with the same weapon."

Author Unknown

406. "The man who will use his skill and constructive imagination to see how much he can give for a dollar, instead of how little he can give for a dollar, is bound to succeed."

Henry Ford (Industrialist)

407. "Success seems to be connected with action. Successful people keep moving. They make mistakes but they never quit."

Conrad Hilton (Hotelier)

Service

408. "What the world lacks most today is men who occupy themselves with the needs of other men. In this unselfish labor a blessing falls on both the helper and the helped."

Albert Schweitzer (German Physician & Philosopher)

409. "The best way to find yourself is to lose yourself in the service of others."

Mahatma Gandhi (Civil Rights Leader & Activist)

410. "Your needs will be met once you can find a way of projecting energy and fulfilling someone else's need."

Stuart Wilde (British Writer)

411. "You are what you do, not what you say you'll do."

Carl Jung (Swiss Psychotherapist & Psychiatrist)

412. "If I look at the mass, I will never act. If I look at the one, I will."

Mother Teresa (Catholic Missionary)

413. "Start where you are. Distant fields always look greener, but opportunity lies right where you are. Take advantage of every opportunity of service."

Robert Collier (Author)

414. "Business is not just doing deals; business is having great products, doing great engineering, and providing tremendous service to customers. Finally, business is a cobweb of human relationships."

Ross Perot (Businessman)

Simplicity

415. "An amazing thing, the human brain. Capable of understanding incredibly complex and intricate concepts. Yet at times unable to recognize the obvious and simple."

Jay Abraham (CEO & Marketing Executive)

416. "The height of cultivation runs to simplicity. Halfway cultivation runs to ornamentation."

Bruce Lee (Martial Artist & Philosopher)

417. "If you can't explain it to a six year old, you don't understand it yourself."

Albert Einstein (German Physicist)

418. "Life is really simple, but we insist on making it complicated."

Confucius (Chinese Philosopher)

419. "Our life is frittered away by detail. Simplify, simplify."

Henry David Thoreau (19th Century American Writer & Philosopher)

420. "The greatest ideas are the simplest."

William Golding (Novelist)

421. "Nature is with simplicity. And nature is no dummy."

Isaac Newton (Physicist)

422. "Simplicity is the ultimate sophistication."

Leonardo da Vinci (Italian Artist & Inventor)

Success

423. "There is no scientific answer for success. You can't define it. You've simply got to live it and do it."

Anita Roddick (Entrepreneur)

424. "Optimism is the one quality more associated with success and happiness than any other."

Brian Tracy (Entrepreneur & Speaker)

425. "Success is not the key to happiness. Happiness is the key to success. If you love what you are doing, you will be successful."

Albert Schweitzer (German Physician & Philosopher)

426. "Failure is the opportunity to begin again, more intelligently."

Henry Ford (Industrialist)

427. "Each success only buys an admission ticket to a more difficult problem."

Henry Kissinger (Diplomat)

428. "Four things for success: work and pray, think and believe."

Norman Vincent Peale (Minister & Author)

429. "Success is getting what you want; happiness is wanting what you get."

Dave Gardner (Comedian)

430. "Success is often achieved by those who don't know that failure is inevitable."

Coco Chanel (French Fashion Designer)

431. "The only certain means of success is to render more and better service than is expected of you, no matter what your task may be."

Og Mandino (Author)

432. "There is only one way to succeed in anything and that is to give it everything."

Vince Lombardi (American Football Coach)

433. "Those who are humble and ambitious are destined for success."

Joe Weider (Publisher & Health Advocate)

434. "The best way to succeed is to double your failure rate."

Thomas J. Watson (American Businessman)

435. "I couldn't wait for success, so I went ahead without it."

Jonathan Winters (Comedian)

436. "Success is never final."

Author Unknown

437. "I've failed over and over and over again in my life and that is why I succeed."

Michael Jordan (Basketball Player)

438. "What is success? I think it is a flair for the thing that you are doing; knowing that it is not enough, that you have got to have hard work and a certain sense of purpose."

Margaret Thatcher (British Prime Minister)

Talent

439. "To do easily what is difficult for others is the mark of talent. To do what is impossible for talent is the mark of genius."

Henri-Frederic Amiel (Swiss Philosopher)

440. "Every artist was first an amateur."

Ralph Waldo Emerson (19th Century Writer)

441. "Talent hits a target no one else can hit. Genius hits a target no one else can see."

Arthur Schopenhauer (Polish Philosopher)

442. "Achievement is talent plus preparation."

Malcolm Gladwell (Writer)

443. "Talent is a wonderful thing, but it won't carry a quitter."

Stephen King (Writer)

444. "Talent is God given. Be humble. Fame is man-given. Be grateful. Conceit is self-given. Be careful."

John Wooden (Basketball Coach)

445. "Genius is talent set on fire by courage."

Henry Van Dyke (American Poet)

Teamwork

446. "Interdependent people combine their own efforts with the efforts of others to achieve their greatest success."

Stephen R. Covey (Educator & Author)

447. "If everyone is moving forward together, then success takes care of itself."

Henry Ford (Industrialist)

448. "It takes two flints to make a fire."

Louisa May Alcott (19th Century American Author)

449. "Teamwork is so important that it is virtually impossible for you to reach the heights of your capabilities or make the money that you want without becoming very good at it."

Brian Tracy (Entrepreneur & Speaker)

Thoughts

450. "During my 87 years, I have witnessed a whole succession of technological revolutions. But none of them has done away with the need for character in the individual or the ability to think."

Bernard Baruch (American Businessman & Statesman)

451. "The world we live in is vastly different from the world we think we live in."

Nassim Nicholas Taleb (Lebanese Scientist & Philosopher)

452. "Life consists in what man is thinking of all day."

Ralph Waldo Emerson (19th Century American Writer)

453. "It is good to be solitary, for solitude is difficult; that something is difficult must be a reason more for us to do it."

Rainer Maria Rilke (Austrian Poet & Novelist)

454. "It is the mark of an educated mind to be able to entertain a thought without accepting it."

Aristotle (Greek Philosopher)

455. "The greatest weapon against stress is our ability to choose one thought over the other."

William James (Philosopher & Psychologist)

Time Management

456. "Time is at once the most valuable and most perishable of all our possessions."

John Randolph (Actor)

457. "Spend the afternoon. You can't take it with you."

Annie Dillard (Author)

458. "Until we can manage time, we can manage nothing else."

Peter F. Drucker (Management Consultant & Author)

459. "I can use my time much better working on tomorrow's problem than fretting about yesterday's."

Ernest J. King (U.S. Navy Admiral)

460. "You must master your time rather than becoming a slave to the constant flow of events and demands on your time. And you must organize your life to achieve balance, harmony, and inner peace."

Brian Tracy (Entrepreneur & Speaker)

461. "Procrastination is the art of keeping up with yesterday."

Don Marquis (American Humorist)

462. "A life devoted to trifles, not only takes away the inclination, but the capacity for higher pursuits."

Hannah More (English Playwright)

463. "Take all the swift advantage of the hours."

William Shakespeare (English Poet & Playwright)

464. "What would be the use of immortality to a person who cannot use well an half hour."

Ralph Waldo Emerson (19th Century American Writer)

Vision

465. "Man is an imagining being."

Gaston Bachelard (French Philosopher)

466. "Formulate and stamp indelibly on your mind a mental picture of yourself as succeeding. Hold this picture tenaciously. Never permit it to fade. Your mind will seek to develop the picture."

Norman Vincent Peale (Minister & Author)

467. "Cherish your visions and your dreams, as they are the children of your soul, the blueprints of your ultimate achievements."

Napoleon Hill (Writer & Speaker)

468. "The future you see is the future you get."

Robert G. Allen (American Businessman & Politician)

469. "In a completely sane world, madness is the only freedom!"

James Graham Ballard (English Novelist & Writer)

470. "A clear vision, backed by definite plans, gives you a tremendous feeling of confidence and personal power."

Brian Tracy (Entrepreneur & Speaker)

471. "Without compelling cause, our employees are just putting in time. Their minds might be engaged, but their hearts are not. Meaning precedes motivation."

Lee J. Colan (Management Consultant)

472. "Nurture your mind with great thoughts for you will never go any higher than you think."

Benjamin Disraeli (19th Century British Prime Minister)

473. "Vision is the art of seeing things invisible."

Jonathan Swift (Irish Poet)

474. "Destiny is not a matter of chance, it's a matter of choice; it is not a thing to be waited for, it is a thing to be achieved."

William Jennings Bryan (American Politician)

Wealth

475. "You can't get a pay raise when you're angry. People will react to the negative energy and will resist you."

Stuart Wilde (Writer)

476. "Wisdom outweighs any wealth."

Sophocles (Greek Playwright)

477. "All the breaks you need in life wait within your imagination. Imagination is the workshop of your mind, capable of turning mind energy into accomplishment and wealth."

Napoleon Hill (Writer & Speaker)

478. "Wealth consists not in having great possessions, but in having few wants."

Epictetus (Greek Philosopher)

479. "We make a living by what we get. We make a life by what we give."

Winston Churchill (British Statesman, Prime Minister & Writer)

480. "Wealth is the slave of a wise man. The master of a fool."

Seneca (Roman Philosopher & Statesman)

481. "The person who doesn't know where his next dollar is coming from usually doesn't know where his last dollar went."

Author Unknown

482. "Empty pockets never held anyone back. Only empty heads and empty hearts can do that."

Norman Vincent Peale (Minister & Author)

Wisdom

483. "To be conscious that you are ignorant of the facts is a great step to knowledge."

Benjamin Disraeli (19th Century British Prime Minister)

484. "It is good even for old men to learn wisdom."

Aeschylus (Greek Playwright)

485. "Wise people learn not to dread but actually to welcome problems because it is in this whole process of meeting and solving problems that life has its meaning."

M. Scott Peck (Psychiatrist & Author)

486. "A wise man can learn more from a foolish question than a fool can learn from a wise answer."

Bruce Lee (Martial Artist & Philosopher)

487. "The art of being wise is the art of knowing what to overlook."

William James (Philosopher & Psychologist)

488. "A fool sees not the same tree that a wise man sees."

William Blake (English Poet & Painter)

489. "If a man will begin with certainties, he shall end in doubts, but if he will be content to begin with doubts, he shall end in certainties."

Francis Bacon (English Writer & Scientist)

490. "Life cannot be administered by definite rules and regulations; that wisdom to deal with a man's difficulties comes only through some knowledge of his life and habits as a whole."

Jane Addams (American Author & Activist)

491. "Turn your wounds into wisdom."

Oprah Winfrey (Talk Show Host & Media Mogul)

492. "To know anything well involves a profound sensation of ignorance."

John Ruskin (Philanthropist & Art Critic)

493. "When a man with money meets a man with experience, the man with money gets experience and the man with experience gets the money."

William Knudsen (American Business Executive)

494. "Knowledge is of no value unless you put it into practice."

Anton Chekhov (Russian Writer)

495. "Next to acquiring good friends, the best acquisition is that of a good book."

Charles Caleb Colton (English Writer)

496. "Knowing thyself is the height of wisdom."

Socrates (Greek Philosopher)

Work

497. "Doin' nothin's a dangerous occupation."

Robert Bolt (Playwright & Screenwriter)

498. "If you will let me, I will wish you in your future what all men desire - enough work to do, and strength enough to do your work."

Rudyard Kipling (English Novelist)

499. "If people knew how hard I worked to gain my mastery, it wouldn't seem so wonderful."

Michelangelo (Italian Artist)

500. "Nobody's a natural. You work hard to get good and then work to get better. It's hard to stay on top."

Paul Coffey (Hockey Player)

501. "What ever you do, do it well. Do it so well that when people see you do it they will want to come back and see you do it again and they will want to bring others and show them how well you do what you do."

Walt Disney (Entertainment Entrepreneur)

502. "Work is not man's punishment. It is his reward and his strength and his pleasure."

George Sand (19th Century French Novelist)

503. "Miracles sometimes occur, but one has to work terribly hard for them."

Chaim Weizmann (Israeli Statesman)

504. "No one should retire from work. If he does, he will shrivel up into a nuisance - talking to everybody about pains and pills and income tax. When I'm not working, I get tired of myself."

Herbert Hoover (U.S. President)

505. "Talent is cheaper than table salt. What separates the talented individual from the successful one is a lot of hard work."

Stephen King (Writer)

506. "Luck is a dividend of sweat. The more you sweat, the luckier you get."

Ray Kroc (Business Executive)

507. "The happiness of men consists in life. And life is in labor."

Leo Tolstoy (Russian Novelist)

508. "Always take a job that's too big for you, and then do your best."

Harry Emerson Fosdick (American Pastor)

509. "A lot of people want a shortcut. I find the best shortcut is the long way, which is basically two words: work hard."

Randy Pausch (American Professor & Lecturer)

510. "Hard work is a prison sentence only if it does not have meaning. Once it does, it becomes the kind of thing that makes you grab your wife around the waist and dance a jig."

Malcolm Gladwell (Writer)

511. "I find my greatest pleasure, and so my reward, in the work that precedes what the world calls success."

Thomas Edison (Inventor & Businessman)

512. "Nobody in life gets exactly what they thought they were going to get. But if you work really hard and you're kind, amazing things will happen."

Conan O'Brien (American Talk Show Host)

About the Compiler

Cameron M. Clark is a business development manager for a professional services company in Las Vegas, Nevada. He holds a Bachelors of Science in Communications from Southern Utah University. He and his wife, Cara are the parents of three children.